James Paul Lewis was born on December 18, 1935 in Little Rock, Arkansas. He was the 5th boy born to Opal Davis Lewis and Lee Lewis. After Paul, along came three sisters and 2 more brothers. Paul grew up with his 9 siblings in Arkansas where he went to school and served at Church.

Paul went on to graduate from Ouachita Baptist University and then Golden Gate Seminary in Mill Valley, California. He was ordained at Crystal Valley Baptist Church in 1955 at the age of 20. He met his wife Ann Craig at a youth rally in Fairfield, California. They were married on June 10, 1961.

Paul has been a minister and pastor for over 60 years at several churches. He helped start over 25 churches in Arizona, Wyoming, Arkansas and Nevada. He was also the Director of Missions for The Southern Baptist Association in Wyoming for 16 years. Ann and Paul have been married for 54 years and have four sons, Tim, Dave, Tony and Dan. They have 4 wonderful daughters-in-law, 10 grandchildren and one great grandson. All of who have inherited a piece of Paul's sense of humor and love for others.

His greatest achievement can be seen in those he has met. Paul is relentlessly encouraging, and like the apostle Paul, unable to stop himself from sharing Jesus with everyone he meets. He loves reading, gardening, and maintains the many friendships he has developed over the years. Paul has spent a great deal of time studying and reading the Bible and has spent his life watching the Bible's promises come to life in his own life. His wish in writing these devotions stem from truth which he has experienced firsthand through his own learning to trust God's perfect peace every day.

PEACE PASSAGES
By J. Paul Lewis

TABLE OF CONTENTS:

*All Scripture is from the New Living Translation (NLT) unless otherwise noted.

4

PEACE PASSAGES

Galatians 5:22, *"But when the Holy Spirit controls our lives, He will produce this kind of fruit in us: love, joy, peace, patience, kindness, goodness, faithfulness, gentleness and self-control...."*

All of these listed fruits of the Holy Spirit are connected. You can't really have one of them without having the others. Certainly when you have genuine peace you will have the others. Now, all of us would like to have peace all the time and God wants us to have it. But peace at any price is not real. A selfish ambition for peace can be dangerous. God wants us to have His peace even when the world is at war, talking and preparing for war. And even when all around us, homes, world systems, politics, jobs, and maybe our own health and security is in unrest and jeopardy, we can still have God's peace.

The key to these fruits being produced in our lives is to submit to the Holy Spirit. When He is in control He constantly calls our attention to Jesus, Who is the Vine that produces these fruits as we abide in Him. The Bible says we grieve The Spirit when we do not submit to Him. I heard of a little boy at school telling his friend that he had learned a simple way to always get along with his parents. He said, "When they tell me what to do, I just do it." And Oh the freedom we have and the peace we have when we just submit to God and do what He says.

It is very important to God and should be to us that we have ongoing peace in our lives. God knows that we cannot effectively worship and serve Him without His peace. An old hymn says, "Trust and obey, for there's no other way, to be happy in Jesus, but to trust and obey." We do this by staying in His Word and submitting to the leadership of His Spirit. In the following I have listed and commented on peace passages in the Bible which God has used and still uses to bring me closer to Him in all the circumstances of life.

I have intentionally kept the comments on these peace passages brief. That has proved to be very difficult as every time I meditate on them I think of different truths in them. This is very true according to circumstances in my life and in the world at the time. It is my hope and prayer that these comments will bless and encourage readers and lead them to a deeper study and meditation on truths of the passages. The passages and comments may also be used in small study groups.

REFLECTIONS:

_____

_____

_____

_____

_____

_____

_____

_____

_____

_____

_____

_____

_____

_____

_____

REFLECTIONS:

_____

_____

_____

_____

_____

_____

_____

_____

_____

_____

_____

_____

_____

_____

_____

_____

THE GIFT OF PEACE

John 14:27, *"I am leaving you with a gift - peace of mind and heart. And the peace I give isn't like the peace the world gives. So don't be troubled or afraid."*

Peace with God is given to us when we believe and receive Jesus Christ into our hearts for the forgiveness of our sins and as the Lord of our lives. It means that you know there was a time in your life when you became convicted by the Holy Spirit that you were a lost sinner. You prayed and asked God to forgive you for your sins. You know you believed Jesus died for your sins and you received Him into your heart. You know now that you belong to God and your desire is to obey Him for the rest of your life on earth. The peace of God is available to each of His children throughout our lives. As we commune with Jesus He offers us His peace for each day; and for each circumstance in our lives. His peace is a gift. As peace with God comes by trusting Him for eternal life, the peace of God comes by trusting Him each step of the way on this earth.

Well, how do you have the peace of God when the world seems to be falling apart and also when your world seems to be falling apart? At times, all of us have needed to know our Lord whispers, "Peace, be still" to the angry storms in our lives. And they will come again. In John 14 Jesus is offering His peace to His first disciples in the midst of difficult times for them and Him. He begins by telling them to not be troubled, and that He will always take care of them. He promised them that

9

when He left them He would continue to be with them in the Holy Spirit. He wanted them to be comforted by the certain knowledge that His Spirit would live in them. He wanted them to know that He would live again after He died for them and that they would live again, too.

 His peace is not like the peace the world offers. The world's peace is based on health, wealth and how things are going in our lives. That peace is not real and we know it doesn't last. God's peace is the same peace that Jesus has. He is the blessed controller of all things in our lives. All in this world will crumble and perish. That's why Jesus tells us in Matthew 6:20-21, *"Store your treasures in Heaven, where they will never become moth-eaten or rusty and where they will be safe from thieves. Wherever your treasure is, there your heart and thoughts will also be."*

We should begin every day by praying for and accepting God's peace for us and others. We should greet each other and relate to each person we meet in the Spirit of God's peace. Most of the time when any troublesome situation arises I pray then for God's peace to dominate my thoughts and actions. I sometimes haven't and then wish I had. Remember, God's peace is His gift to us. We can't work for it or do anything to earn it. It is not based on whether we always do right or make right decisions. He never takes it back. In troubles and difficulties we sometimes forget and panic, but it's always there for us.

When I pray this verse in John 14:27 I say something like, "Lord I thank you for your gift of peace. I thank you that I don't have to do anything and that I can't do anything to have your peace. Thank you that it is not like the world's so called peace. If all else be gone, your peace remains forever. That's all I need. I accept and receive your peace anew now for this day and for this present situation. Thank you Lord."

> # We should begin every day by praying for and accepting God's peace for us and others.

REFLECTIONS:

PEACE FROM THE LORD OF PEACE

2 Thessalonians 3:16, *"May the Lord of peace Himself always give you His peace no matter what happens. The Lord be with you all."*

They already had peace with God. Paul prays for them to have the peace of the Lord in all things. When you know "the Lord of peace" you know the Lord's peace. The Lord of peace wants us to always have His peace "no matter what happens." We try to not think of all the things that could happen to us. When I think of some of the many terrible and tragic things that have happened to people close to me or things I hear about on the news daily, I sometimes think there would be no way I would be able to endure them. And it is true that by myself I could not. The one reason I know I could is that the Lord of peace would be with me.

  When I was a young pastor I remember when I first received calls telling of things like the tragic death of a child or other terrible happenings in the community. As I made my way to visit with the families I would feel so helpless with thoughts that there was no way I could be able to go through that in my own life. I would try to think of what I could say or do to help in the situation. When the families did not know God or were not close to Him it would be very difficult, though some of the times the people were open to hearing about the peace and comfort the Lord offered. Through the years I have seen many people come to know the Lord and have peace with Christ Jesus through these circumstances.

13

But many times when I arrived to try to comfort and tell of God's peace for people going through tragic events, I would find that the Lord was already there, giving amazing grace and peace to His people. I remember that at those times I was the one who was comforted the most. I was given peace by the Lord through the words of peace and love from those who had suffered loss.

God does offer peace for anything that happens in our lives. He wants us to claim it in everything that happens and to know we will have His peace throughout our lives here. Paul prayed for this peace for the Thessalonian Christians. We should pray this every day for each other. We have peace with God because we've received Jesus as the Savior and leader of our lives. We are to pray as Paul did, that we will all have the peace of the Lord everyday and in all that happens in our lives.

Today I pray, "Thank you Lord that you really are the Lord of Peace. You have blessed me so greatly in so many ways. Today things are going real good for me and I don't see any trouble on my horizon. Still, I am consciously aware of the need for your peace. It's sure good to know that though I don't know what will happen, You do know, and as you promised you are going to see that it all works together for my good. The best thing I know is that you will be with me as always. I pray that you will be with my family and others today and that they will know it and give thanks to you." I then continue to pray and praise Him.

14

When you know "the Lord of peace" you know the Lord's peace.

REFLECTIONS:

_____

_____

_____

_____

_____

_____

_____

_____

_____

_____

_____

_____

_____

_____

PEACE IN KNOWING YOU HAVE ETERNAL LIFE

1 John 5:12-13, "He who has the Son has life; he who does not have the Son of God does not have life. I have written these things to you who believe in the name of the Son of God so that you may know that you have eternal life." (NIV)

People who have known me through the years know that I love to share the Good News of eternal life in Jesus to people on a person to person basis. I've shared by using gospel tracts in booklet form. I've shared by using what is known as the Roman road, where several verses in the book of Romans are used. I've used what is referred to as the bridge illustration, and I've shared my personal testimony many times, using John 3:16 and other Bible verses. There have also been many times that I've explained ways of presenting the gospel as I've taught courses on witnessing. Whatever the approach, it should be simple and usually brief so a little child can understand.

My favorite way of sharing is by using 1 John 5:12-13. For me it is the easiest to present and to be understood. It is the simplest and the least time consuming way. Here it is: After I've received permission to share I begin by saying, "I'm going to make a statement to you that is very true and is stated in the Bible. Before God there are two groups of people in the world. There are those who are saved and have eternal life and those who are lost and do not have eternal life. Now let's read this in the Bible." I turn to 1 John 5:12-13 and read it while the person I'm conversing with is able to see it and read along with me. I then say, "Now do you believe the Bible is the Word of God and that this is what it is telling us about having eternal life?" When the person agrees I then continue. In the course of the presentation I will ask if the person is agreeing to that point. I will not include that in this account but will explain it as I do in the presentation.

The Bible says here and throughout the Bible that the difference in the two groups of people is that people in one group have eternal life because they have believed in the Name of Jesus, the Son of God. So, it is very important for us to know what it means to believe in the Name of Jesus. If you believed in my name it would mean you believe I am who I say I am and I will keep my word if I tell you something. I want people to believe that about me but I know I'm not perfect. Jesus is the perfect Son of God. To believe in His Name means you believe He is who the Bible says He is. He is the One who loved you so much that He died for your sins on the cross. He is so powerful that He conquered death and arose from the grave. The Bible says here that anyone who believes in Him and invites Him into his or her heart will know their sins are forgiven and that they have eternal life right now. Their bodies will die but they will live forever with God in the Heaven that He is preparing for us.

When the person says he understands and does believe in the Name of Jesus I say, "Now, the Bible says when you believe in the Name of Jesus you will want to call on His Name and invite Him to come into your heart. Let's turn to Romans 10:13 and read. Here the Bible says that *"Anyone who calls on the Name of the Lord will be saved.* To be saved means our sins are forgiven and we have eternal life from now on." I then say, "Would you be willing to right now call on the Name of Jesus and ask Him to forgive you of your sins and be the leader of your life from now on?" If the person says "yes" I usually offer to lead him in the simple prayer calling on Jesus to forgive him and give him eternal life. When he has prayed I welcome him into the family of God and lead in a prayer thanking God. I then tell him of the support I will give to him and others will give to him on his new journey. I remind him that God's Word says that now he can know he is a child of God and has eternal life because he has believed in the Name of Jesus and called on His Name to save Him. I give him material that explains what baptism means and other things that are important in beginning his new life.

This discourse most of the time takes only a few minutes. The outcomes will vary but that is not up to you. If the person decides not to pray and receive Jesus right then, I try to leave the door open and encourage him to make the decision and pray to receive Christ soon. I assure him that I will be his friend and other Christians will be there when he needs us.

Prayer: "Dear Lord, we know that you are the way, the truth, and the life. We know that nobody will enter your kingdom without calling on your name and receiving you into their hearts. We know that it is your will that each of your children seeks to actively share our faith in you with others.   I pray that you will work through me and others in any way you want to share the Good News of life in your Name."

He is the One who loved you so much that He died for your sins on the cross.

REFLECTIONS:

_____

_____

_____

_____

_____

_____

_____

_____

_____

_____

_____

_____

_____

_____

REFLECTIONS:

PEACE IN TIMES OF TROUBLE

Psalm 46:1-2, *"God is our refuge and strength, always ready to help in times of trouble. So we will not fear, even if earthquakes come and the mountains crumble into the sea."*

What great comforting words these are, assuring us that God is our refuge and strength in any circumstance of life. There is no safe refuge on Earth for what is described here. For the things happening in the world today and for things that will happen eventually, there is no safe refuge on Earth. And for the things that happen and may happen in our lives, there is no safe refuge and strength in the things of this world. These words from an old hymn are so true, "Other refuge have I none, hangs my helpless soul on Thee." All possible places of refuge in the world have crumbled and will crumble.

Nothing and nobody is stronger than God. All the forces and powers in the universe were made and are controlled by Him. Like a human parent watching over his child, our awesome all-powerful God is constantly watching over His children. And our Heavenly Father has all power. But why is He watching us? He is ever ready to come to our rescue when we get in trouble. Now for Christians He not only watches over us. He lives in us in the Holy Spirit to guide, strengthen, comfort us, and to give us everything we need for any time.

When these difficult times come, as they will for each of us, it is good to be reminded that nothing takes God by surprise. He knows His plans for us and they are for our good no matter what happens.

I recently read in Proverbs 16:9, *"We can make our plans, but the Lord determines our steps."* I don't know where it came from but later that day I thought of this old saying, "We plan. God laughs." When that thought came at first I laughed. Then I was sobered. I then felt like laughing and crying at the same time. Like laughing with joy that God really was in control and always takes care of me. I felt like crying with sorrow that I too often panic at first before accepting His control and loving care for me.

Now, whenever trials and sufferings or any difficulties happen we probably will at first fear. But we don't continue to be afraid when we hear the Holy Spirit assure us that God is in control and He is taking care of us. Where is our powerful awesome God when troubles come into our lives? He is here with us as our refuge and strength. God is present with us at all times. We know we really need Him with us, all the time. But His presence is manifested and real to us more so when we call on Him in times of trouble in our lives.

Pray with me as we are guided by these verses. "Dear Lord, thank you for the peace we have in knowledge that you are our refuge and strength. You always are with us and ready to help in times of trouble. We know there is no reason for us to fear, no matter what happens. Help us to believe it and live it.

Where is our powerful awesome God when troubles come into our lives? He is here with us as our refuge and strength. God is present with us at all times.

REFLECTIONS:

PEACE IN KNOWING GOD IS IN CONTROL

Psalm 46:10, *"Be silent and know that I am God! I will be honored by every nation.   I will be honored throughout the world."*

God is in control of the nations, the world, and in my life. In experiencing Him I am to forget my program and get with His program, His plan, and His purpose for my life. I don't need to tell Him anything. I am to listen to Him by His Spirit speaking His Word to my heart. I once heard a preacher say that there were two very important things each person should learn early in life and remember them for the rest of His life: He said the first thing to learn is that there is a God, and the second is that you are not Him. I thought that is so true but I wish God didn't have to remind me of it so often. So, Psalm 46:10 is a wonderful, exciting promise. In it God says that the victory is already won and He is in perfect control of us and all we do as we live for Him.

As we see daily the terrible troubles in the nations and obviously many more troubles on the horizon we are to watch quietly, wait and to know He knows everything about everything that is happening and that will happen. Also we will see difficulties and sufferings come into our lives and know that as we continue to live in the world, more will come.   Then we can know that the same awesome all-powerful and loving God who is in control of the world and the nations is certainly in control as our refuge and strength at all times.

27

To me many signs and Bible prophecy fulfillments indicate the soon coming again of Christ when our salvation will be consummated. Christians are not be troubled by the times in which we live.

Rather, we are to be excited and hopeful with great expectation. In chapter 21 of Luke Jesus tells of many of the conditions that will exist near the time of His coming back. Then In Luke 21:28, He says, *"So when all these things begin to happen, stand straight and look up, for your salvation is near."*

In 1 Thessalonians 4, after a wonderful discourse on the certainty of our resurrection and of the coming again of the Lord, when we *"will be caught up in the clouds to meet the Lord in the air and remain with Him forever,"* Paul said in verse 18, *"so comfort and encourage each other with these words."* We are to live on this Earth in victory and joy. We also are to daily look forward to His return with great joy. In Revelation 22:20 John quotes Jesus as saying, *"Yes, I am coming soon."* And John replies, *"Amen. Come, Lord Jesus."*

Prayer: "Lord, thank you that you are in total control of the nations and of the world. To us who belong to you, you are in perfect control of our lives. You love us and take care of us. Help us to daily submit to your will for us. You do use us and will continue to use us in your service. But you do not need our help. You only want our trust in you. Some day you will make everything right and holy. You will be honored by people from all the nations of the world."

The first thing to learn is that there is a God, and the second is that you are not Him.

REFLECTIONS:

PEACE THAT NEVER LETS GO

Hebrews 13:5-6, *"Stay away from the love of money; be satisfied with what you have. For God has said, I will never fail you. I will never forsake you. That is why we can say with confidence, The Lord is my helper, so I will not be afraid. What can mere mortals do to me?"*

Here God says that we are to be free from the love of money, and to be content with what we have. He means that whether we have a lot of possessions, a little, or not any, we are not to be enslaved by them. God sets us free from all fears. But many Christians are still in bondage by the love of money. That means we want more, or are afraid we may lose what we have. We are instructed to daily trust in the Lord our helper, not in money or anything in this perishing world. If we don't, we lose God's peace and may be disciplined in God's love.

Assurance of Gods presence in our lives assures the absence of fear. When we know without doubt that He is present we have nothing but peace. God is with me all the time. Through the years I've loved the old song, "My Lord is with me all the time." It must be old and it must have been written for me since it was written in my birth year, 1935. Of course the message is for all who know Christ. The writer says, "In the lighting flash across the sky His mighty power I see, And I know if He can reign on high, His light can shine on me. I've seen it in the lighting, heard it in the thunder, and felt it in the rain; My Lord is with me all the time." When I was a missionary in Wyoming and drove across the mountains and high plains in the winter, I wrote this verse to that song, "When the blizzard sweeps across the plains and chills the body cold, then His love within me gives me peace, His love and care to know. My Lord is with me all the Time." In all weather conditions and in all situations He is always with us.

After Jesus commissioned His first disciples and sent them out to proclaim His Good News he told them in Matthew 28:20, *"And be sure of this: I am with you always, even to the end of the age."* That promise has never been and never will be rescinded. I thank God that great songs of trust in Christ are still being written and sung today. I love this one written by Matt and Beth Redman in 2005, "Even though I walk through the valley of the shadow of death, your perfect love is casting out fear. And even when I'm caught in the middle of the storms of this life, I won't turn back, I know you are near. And I will fear no evil, for my God is with me. And if my God is with me, whom then shall I fear? Oh no, you never let go, through the calm and through the storm. Oh no, You never let go, in every high and every low. Oh no, You never let go. Lord, You never let go of me."

There are so many things in this world to be afraid of, and things to fear are increasing every day. Someone has said, if you are not afraid in the world today it may be that you just don't understand the situation. But for those who trust in God, we can understand what is going on OR NOT and still have perfect peace in Him. God will keep us in His peace as we live in His Spirit and in His Word. So, whatever we may fear today whether it be failure, rejection, illness or physical danger, turn it over to God in prayer and faith in His Word. Memorize passages on peace and meditate on them. The Spirit will bring them to your attention when you need them the most. Psalm 27:1 has blessed me so many times, *"The Lord is my light and my salvation – whom shall I fear? The Lord is the stronghold of my life – of whom shall I be afraid."* NIV

Prayer: "Lord, help us to be thankful to you for things you have given to us. We only need you. We don't have to be afraid. We don't have to covet more things. We are confident that you will never leave us. You are our helper. Nothing or no one can hurt us. In you we are not afraid."

We can understand what is going on OR NOT and still have perfect peace in Him.

God will keep us in His peace as we live in His Spirit and in His Word. So, whatever we may fear today whether it's failure, rejection, illness or physical danger turn it over to God in prayer and faith in His Word. Memorize passages on peace and meditate on them. The Spirit will bring them to your attention when you need them the most.

REFLECTIONS:

REFLECTIONS:

GOD'S JOYFUL PEACE

John 15:11, *"I have told you this so that you will be filled with my joy. Yes, your joy will overflow.*

We have the Joy of Jesus by staying closely connected to Him each day and in all the circumstances of our lives. We become weak when we forget and stray away from Him.   The greatest joy comes in a close intimate relationship with Him. In the verses preceding verse 11 Jesus tells us to just continue to abide in Him and we will have His joy in us.   His victorious peace and fruitfulness becomes ours in a great overflowing joy that blesses Him, us and others.

Jesus wants me to be filled with His joy.   I seek the fullness of His joy in my relationship with Him. Certainly He is full of great joy and He wants me to have fullness of Joy in Him. That is peace. He is always full of joy. He never worries.   He wants the same for me and for each of us. It isn't that He is not concerned and doesn't care. No one cares like Jesus. But He knows everything will be okay. I do, too, as the focus of my attention is on Him.

Jesus wants us to keep God's commandments and live right because He knows if we don't we will lose His joy. He also knows if we are not joyful in Him we won't serve Him from our hearts.   David said in Psalm 51:12-13, *"Restore to me again the joy of your salvation, and make me willing to obey you.   Then I will teach your ways to sinners and they will return to you."* Others will

37

only believe our witness when they see the joy of knowing the Lord in us.

God's word says in Nehemiah 8:10, *"The joy of the Lord is your strength."* When a person becomes a follower of Christ, God does not promise a life on easy street, free of trials, troubles, suffering and temptations. Life will not be perfect. In fact God calls us to a battleground. The devil and evil will battle us fiercely.

When a Christian has the joy of the Lord alive in Him, he is a strong loving Christian. And he doesn't go around with his head hanging down in despair. He doesn't have time to complain or fuss. He is busy praising and serving God joyfully, even in persecution and suffering. Committed to serving God, the disciple of Christ discovers that *"the joy of the Lord is your (our) strength."*

Yes, the joy of the Lord will be our strength throughout our lives. It will especially be our strength when we are dying. I hate sad songs about death. It is only sad when one dies if they don't know the Lord. I've seen many people die. What a difference it is when they know Jesus.

Pray with me, "Father, I can't thank and praise you enough for your overflowing joy in all the circumstances of my life. I pray that others will see it and know it is you and that they can have it, too."

Others will only believe our witness when they see the joy of knowing the Lord in us.

REFLECTIONS:

_____

_____

_____

_____

_____

_____

_____

_____

_____

_____

_____

_____

_____

_____

_____

_____

_____

FELLOWSHIP OF PEACE AND JOY

2 John 12, *"Well, I have much more to say you, but I don't want to say it in a letter. (My comment: Or by email, text message or twitter) For I hope to visit you soon and to talk to you face to face. Then our joy will be complete."*

Here John the beloved apostle says that the fullness of Jesus' joy in each of us is meant to be shared with the fellowship of believers. We need to go the church meetings and Bible Study groups regularly and to share what God is doing in our lives with others. God desires us to make a long term commitment to the fellowship of God's people in the church He places us in. In these days Christians need each other more than ever. God instructs us in Hebrews 10:25, *"And let us not neglect our meeting together, as some people do, but encourage and warn each other, especially now that the day of his coming back again is drawing near."* God said it. We'd better believe it.

The follower of Jesus who stays close to Him realizes the need to have contact with fellow believers in the church God has placed them in. As we meet, we are to express love and encouragement to each other in God's love. This requires forgetting self and time. When anyone begins to miss the worship and fellowship meetings as a pattern and doesn't feel it is needed, that is sinful pride and he is headed for a fall.

41

It is the joy that God gives to us that we share with each other. We share by singing together, praying together, opening up God's word together, hearing His word proclaimed together, speaking love and encouragement to each other and by just being present together in the Spirit of our Lord. Every one of us has faults and failures. We are to constantly look to Jesus as Lord of His church. He is the holy, perfect One. Each of us are still in different stages of development and growth as His children.

John says when God's people get together and fellowship "face to face, then our joy will be complete." What makes our joy complete? It is the fact that it is the joy of the Lord. When we gather to observe His supper we celebrate His sacrifice of His body and blood for the remission of our sins. In the observance, we also commit to bond together in "proclaiming His death until He comes back." We don't observe His supper every time we meet. But every time we meet it should be in the joy of our Lord and in the encouragement and commitment to proclaiming His Good News individually and collectively. Then we go out to our various places in the world with this common purpose. This is the real heart of God. God promises that He will build His Church and maintain the fellowship of peace as we stay near His heart. The old hymn says, "There is a place of full release, near to the heart of God. A place where all is joy and peace, near to the heart of God."

Prayer: "Dear Lord, thank you for letting us be a part of a loving, joyful, caring and sharing church. May I join faithfully in sharing blessings and burdens and listening to others as they share. Your perfect love in each of us will cast out all fear."

As we meet we are to express love and encouragement to each other in God's love. This requires forgetting self and time. When anyone begins to miss the worship and fellowship meetings as a pattern and doesn't feel it is needed, that is sinful pride and he is headed for a fall.

REFLECTIONS:

PRAISE BRINGS PEACE

Psalm 34:1-2, *"I will praise the Lord at all times. I will constantly speak His praises. I will boast only in the Lord: let all who are discouraged take heart."*

Yes, we are at all times to praise the Lord in our hearts, at all times, David, who certainly had his share of trials and suffering, said we are to praise God and speak His praises at all times. I have found many times that I cannot possibly really praise God, and not have peace in all situations. In good times and with good news I most always immediately say, "Praise God." When bad news or uncertainty comes I always say, "Praise God," though usually not as soon. But oh the joy and peace that flows in me and through me even in the midst of suffering and uncertainty when I say from my heart, "PRAISE GOD!"

It is a great joy to go to sleep at night when I'm praising God. It helps me to go to sleep. Then when I wake up during the night I am more likely to be praising God and to go back to sleep soon. It is so much better than waking up with troubles and uncertainties on my mind. When anything else comes to mind I then just think of how great God is and how He has it all under His control. Then I can continue to praise Him. It is so peaceful to focus on the problem controller rather than on the problems. Then I am more likely to wake up in the morning with the continued mind-set of praising God. I am more likely during the day to "constantly speak His praises" in my heart and from my lips as opportunities arise.

45

I like to boast. I think I'm good at it. There I go boasting again. Well, its okay if it is "only in the Lord." What are some things you like to boast about? I like to boast about what a wonderful wife and family God has given to me. I like to say that my grandchildren are better and smarter than the average grandchildren. I like to boast about my church and pastor. You see I believe that God has given me the best in everything. He has entrusted them to me and I am to acknowledge His ownership of them all and to follow His plan for me. When we boast we are to take no credit but to give glory, honor and praise all to Him.

Well, I don't like to get discouraged. But sometimes I do. Praise God that I don't stay that way for a long time. God reminds me of His presence and control in every situation. He reminds me through His Spirit and Bible passages like this Psalm of praise to trust in God. He also reminds us of His presence through encouragement of other caring Christians. I pray that as you are reading this you will read the rest of Psalm 34. Wow! What an uplifting passage! Like this in verses 18-19, *"The Lord is close to the brokenhearted and saves those who are crushed in spirit. A righteous man may have many troubles, but the Lord delivers him from them all."* NIV.

It is a great joy to go to sleep at night when I'm praising God.

46

We should begin each day and continue through the day praising God. Begin each time of prayer by praising God. Praise God when beginning a new relationship and God will guide you in it. Praise Him when you are blessed. Praise Him when you are praised. Praise Him when you are criticized. Praise Him when you may have failed. Praise Him in pain and suffering. Praise Him wherever you are. Praise Him in all you do. He will put things in the right perspective when you praise Him. When you really praise Him, He will lead you in your proceeding thoughts and actions. He will lead you to confess sins. He will lead you to be thankful. You will be released from guilt. He will make things right in your life and relationships. You will be blessed greatly with joy and peace when you truly praise Him from your heart. PRAISE GOD! Try it. You'll like it.

Prayer: "Lord, I want to praise you at all times day and night. As I speak may it be with praise to you in my heart. Help me to boast only in what you have done and will do. When I am discouraged may I take heart in praising you and lead others to praise you."

He will lead you to confess sins. He will lead you to be thankful. You will be released from guilt.
PRAISE GOD!
Try it.
You'll like it!

REFLECTIONS:

_____

_____

_____

_____

_____

_____

_____

_____

_____

_____

_____

_____

_____

_____

_____

_____

REFLECTIONS:

GOD'S SPIRIT BRINGS PEACE, NOT FEAR

2 Timothy 1:7, *"For God has not given us a spirit of fear and timidity, but of power, love and self discipline."*

If we have a spirit of fear it is not the spirit of God. God has given each of His children His Spirit to live in us. Though we are sometimes afraid, His Spirit in us casts it out. Paul wanted to encourage Timothy in the Lord. We all need encouragement. Paul knew Timothy had the Spirit of God in Him and needed to submit to the power of the Spirit in his life and ministry. He didn't tell Timothy to try to have a more positive attitude, to work harder or pray longer. He told him to return to submitting to the peace and power of the Spirit of God living in him.

I think we all know how powerful the devil is. We best not forget it. The Bible says he *"prowls around like a roaring lion, looking for some victim to devour."* (1 Peter 5:8) That is, the devil first makes his prey afraid in order to set them up for destruction. The devil knows he cannot destroy Christians. But he can make us afraid and cause us to lose our peace, influence and witness. A spirit of fear leads us to focus attention on ourselves. There we are inadequate to do what God may lead us to do and say what He wants us to say. If the devil is to impede the progress of God's work in the world he must try to stop Christians for God has chosen to use us to get His good news to the world.

When one gives into a spirit of fear he will see a problem in every opportunity. Paul was led by the Spirit of God, and he saw an opportunity in every problem. In living for Christ in this world we will have problems, troubles, trials and impossible situations. In our own strength we will say we can't do it. As we let God guide us by His Word and by His Spirit He will tell us that is right, we can't do it; but when we trust and follow His Spirit of power in us He will enable us to do whatever He tells us to do. In whatever we face in life we need to pray that we will not try to handle it in our own strength; but that we will surrender to the power of the Holy Spirit and learn to depend on Him. We will have an ample supply of His peace as we rely on His power and timing.

I've heard it said that if it weren't for people we wouldn't have any problems at all. The problems we face in our lives are usually with people. People like spouses, children, neighbors, bosses, church members, etc. People like yourself. You and I are usually our own worst enemies, aren't we? But people are not problems when we love them. The Bible tells us in Luke:27 that we *"must love the Lord your God with all your heart, all your soul, all your strength, and all your mind. And love your neighbor as yourself."* When we have a Spirit of love it means we have the Spirit of God's love flowing through us. We know we are loved by God. Because of His love to us we love ourselves. And it is only because we have received God's love for us that we can reach out to others in love without fear.

"Self-discipline" is one of the fruits of the spirit listed in Galatians 5:22. Now, there is no way we can have a Spirit of self-discipline, or a sound mind, unless the Holy Spirit is in control in our lives. That means we will have what some have called "horse sense," or "stable thinking." But when it's directed by the Spirit of God it even smells good. The Holy Spirit will direct us to follow God's Word. He will give us the mind of Christ so we will think as He thinks. We will see people and situations as He does. We will have His peace and His victory.

The spirit of fear and timidity will not dominate. The Bible says in 1 John 4:4, "*But you belong to God, my dear children. You have already won your fight with these false prophets, because the Spirit who lives in you is greater than the spirit who lives in the world.*" As children of God we still live in this world. We still have to cope with things like   false prophets,   w o r r i e s,   sufferings,   and   other adversaries.   But John admonishes us to be at peace because even though we are still in a fight with the fears of this world, we have the all-powerful victorious Spirit of God living in us and the fight is already won.

Prayer: "Dear Lord, we are your children and we love peace. We would rather avoid battle in this world. But we are in it. The world doesn't like you. It doesn't like us. But it is really exciting and even joyful to be in a battle we know we've already won. In the power, love and right thinking of the Holy Spirit in us we have all we need to endure and be victorious. May we continue to

53

think like this with your mind in us. We thank you for your unfailing love for us. We love you and want to live boldly to give honor, glory and praise to your Name."

REFLECTIONS:

_____

_____

_____

_____

_____

_____

_____

_____

_____

_____

_____

_____

_____

_____

_____

_____

REFLECTIONS:

GOD'S PERFECT PEACE

Isaiah 26:3-4, *"You will keep in perfect peace all who trust in you, whose thoughts are fixed on you. Trust in the Lord always, for the Lord God is the eternal Rock."*

The 26th chapter of Isaiah is a song sung by Judah in the midst of difficult and uncertain times. With all the terrible things happening in and around the land of Judah they could sing this wonderfully beautiful song of victory to those who looked to God and trusted in Him. They attribute their perfect peace to God, their eternal Rock. They knew God was in control and as stated in verse nineteen, "Yet we have this assurance: those who belong to God will live; their bodies will rise again."

God wants to keep us in perfect peace. As children of God we have the assurance of His Word that once we trust Him for our salvation we cannot lose eternal life and standing with Him. Obviously, we can and do sometimes lose His peace because we still have that sinful nature in us. We are assured of having His peace and joy restored to us and of keeping it when our trust is totally in Him. God promises His perfect ongoing peace to those whose thoughts are fixed on Him. It means our thoughts, desires, affections, and emotions are focused on Him. To be in His "perfect" peace means God is foremost in your thoughts and you have turned all things in your life over to Him in total trust. At those times He leads us to just know that He is in control and everything will be okay.

We are to keep our thoughts fixed in God by staying in His Word, reading it, listening to others reading it, meditating on it, praying it, and speaking it to others. God's Word is truth. The Lord God is the eternal, immovable and solid Rock. Quite often thoughts on Bible truths remind me of songs I've sung throughout my life. Here I am reminded of, "My hope is built on nothing less than Jesus' blood and righteousness. I dare not trust the sweetest frame, but wholly lean on Jesus' Name. On Christ the solid Rock I stand. All other ground is sinking sand."

In southeast Wyoming there is a 10,274 foot mountain called Laramie Peak. I would often see it as I drove through Southeast Wyoming visiting churches and pastors. You can see that mountain peak for nearly a hundred miles in any direction. It was a very important landmark for pioneers who used it as a weather indicator and landmark to guide their travel to the west. It was immovable, large and they could always trust it to guide them. As we travel the road of life we will see and experience many difficulties and uncertainties that we have never had before. Even as those pioneers fixed their attention on Laramie Peak for guidance and direction we are to fix our attention on our powerful, immovable, loving and caring God. He will always be there for us in every situation. And He assures us that no matter what happens we are going to make it.

If our trust is totally in the Lord Jesus we are very sure that we are standing on the solid Rock. He is the Rock of our salvation. He is the Stone that the builder rejected. We know the truth of His Word in John 14:6, *"I am the Way and the Truth and the Life. No one comes to the Father except through me."* NIV. There really is a scarlet thread throughout the Bible. The whole Book points to Jesus. We are to fix our attention on Him. He is the living Word of God as we read in John 1:1-18.

I love this promise and treasure it deeply. I couldn't make it without it. As we abide in Him we have perfect calm even in the midst of troubles, sadness, suffering and other turbulences.

In weaknesses, perfect rest in all circumstances, perfect peace in every situation. I've experienced it often, though too often, after I've panicked for awhile and lost it. It is so wonderful that no matter how we respond to troubles, He remains faithful and restores His joy and peace as we call on Him.

Prayer: "Lord Jesus, may I constantly trust in you as I keep my mind fixed on you in all my thoughts, desires, affections, emotions and actions. Thank you for always being faithful to me. I stand on you and abide in you, my eternal Rock."

Jesus Himself is the promise.
He is the perfect peace.

REFLECTIONS:

_____

_____

_____

_____

_____

_____

_____

_____

_____

_____

_____

_____

_____

_____

_____

_____

_____

PEACE IN TRUSTING AND ACKNOWLEDGING GOD IN EVERYTHING

Proverbs 3:5-8, *"Trust in the Lord with all your heart and lean not on your own understanding; in all your ways acknowledge Him, and He will make your paths straight. Do not be wise in your own eyes; fear the Lord and shun evil. This will bring health to your body and nourishment to your bones."* NIV

What a difference it would make if every Christian father would give this kind of instruction to his children as Solomon did to his son. Would you like to have this kind of wisdom to give and to live? Well, Solomon asked God for it so he could use it to honor God, bless his family, and the nation. Now, none of us have any excuse for not having this wisdom. God gives it to each of us who trust Him and want it to serve Him and bring honor and praise to Him. It's right here in the Book of Proverbs, which God has preserved for us for many years. We have the fullness of God's peace as we acknowledge Him in all our ways, following His instructions and not our own understanding.

In these verses Solomon makes it very clear, the way for a young person to have a healthy body and peaceful mind. To live right and straight and have peace in a crooked world, our confidence must not be in ourselves or others. It must not be in institutions, governments, or political leaders of parties. These will eventually crumble and fall. Only God is unchangeable and constantly strong. No one has ever said, "Oh, I wish I

61

had not trusted in God, or I wish I had not put all my trust in Him." Whereas, I have heard many say they wish they had trusted in Christ sooner. The Bible says that when this world is being destroyed and Christ comes back many will say they wish they had trusted God and accepted Christ. But then it will be too late. Solomon would tell his son today to be sure to not be one of those.

When Solomon tells his son to, "not be wise in your own eyes" he is really saying what we need to hear and tell our children in our day; "Son, be wise, but don't be a wise guy." Solomon prayed that above all else God would give him wisdom. God granted that request. He then blessed and used Solomon immensely to bless many others and to give honor to God. Much of the book of Proverbs is addressed directly to Solomon's son. He wanted God's words of wisdom to bless the nation, but he especially wanted his family to hear and follow them. God put them in his heart. He sought to live by them and to pass them onto others. To each of us the message is, "Go and do likewise." We cannot have God's peace in our hearts unless we do.

I often pray these verses in this way, "Lord, help me to trust you with all my heart and to not rely on my own understanding. May I seek, submit to and follow your will for me in all that happens. I will give you glory and praise as you direct my path. I pray you will keep me in a spirit of reverence, submission and respect for you in every decision I make and everything I do.

May I be wise but know it's your wisdom. May I constantly realize that I can do nothing right without you." You can't pray like that and mean it without having God's peace.

REFLECTIONS:

PEACE FROM WORRIES AND CARES

I Peter 5:7, *"Give all your worries and cares to God, for He cares what happens to you."*

Peter writes these words in discussing the right motivation for serving God. In previous verses he had said that we are not to serve God for what we may get out of it, but because we are really eager to serve Him. And he instructs us to serve each other in humility, submitting to God and to each other.

We want to do the right thing about all our worries and cares. That may be what we really worry the most about. Will we do the right thing? The right thing to do is to pray. God invites us in prayer to bring all of our concerns to Him. He already knows about them and what He is going to do about them. Of course it would not be right or realistic for us to not care. But God wants us to talk with Him about them and then to just leave them with Him. When they come back up again in our minds, we are to continue praying, following His direction, and knowing He is taking care of them. We will have and abide in His peace. Whatever happens and whatever He leads us to do will be in His peace.

Paul indicates that all of God's children do sometimes have worries and cares. In order to really give all our worries and cares to God we must be willing to totally trust Him with them. Can we give them to Him? Can we give them all to Him? As Christians we certainly have been set free by Jesus, but sometimes we don't live like

65

it. The key to giving our burdens to Jesus in total trust that He is going to do the right thing with them is to know just how much He really loves us and to live in that love. So, how much does He love us? Paul states it clearly in Romans 8:32, *"He who did not spare His own Son, but gave Him up for us all – how will He not also, along with Him, graciously give us all things?"* NIV

He loved us enough to die for us. If we really believe He loved us that much we will not be afraid to trust our worries and cares to Him. John the Beloved Apostle said in 1 John 4:16, *"And so we know and rely on the love that God has for us. God is love. Whoever lives in love lives in God, and God in Him."* (NIV) If we live in His love then we are not afraid to trust Him and to live for Him. Verse 18 says, *"Such love has no fear because perfect love expels all fear."* Knowing and abiding in God's perfect love means that I don't have to be afraid of anything or anybody in this world. He is in control of my life in the most caring, loving manner. In 1 John, John said God loved us enough to call us His children, *"and that is what we are!"* That is the ultimate in assurance of God's peace in any circumstance of life.

We can confidently say that God really does care what happens to us. It gives us peace to know that He knows what is going to happen to us and knows what He is going to do about it. Oh how wonderful and peaceful it is to know that the God of the whole universe sees and knows whatever happens to us and will see that it all works together for our good. We do not need to begin any day

66

without knowing that God already knows what is going to happen and will take care of us.

Prayer: "Help me to do the right thing about worries and cares. Help me to give them to you. Thank you for being patient with me, forgiving me and continuing to love and care for me when I try to work them out myself before giving them to you. In my heart I know you care about what happens to me and will always take care of me. May I be motivated by your love and care to be eager to serve you. Help me to be an encourager and submit to others because I love you and submit humbly to you."

> We do not need to begin any day without knowing that God already knows what is going to happen and will take care of us.

REFLECTIONS:

_____

_____

_____

_____

_____

_____

_____

_____

_____

_____

_____

_____

_____

_____

_____

_____

THE LIGHT OF THE WORLD BRINGS PEACE

John 8:12, *"Jesus said to the people, I am the light of the world. If you follow me you won't be stumbling through the darkness, because you will have the light that leads to life."*

The world is in the darkness of sin and separation from God. In John 3:19 Jesus said, "The light from heaven came into the world, but they loved the darkness more than light, for their actions were evil." In contrast Jesus said in verse 21, "But those who do what is right gladly come to the light."

Those who follow Christ do go through valleys of suffering, trials and difficulties. But when we go through the trials we don't have to stumble in darkness. When I say something like, "God, I've never been this way or had experiences like this before. I am afraid." Then God whispers His Words to me, "I'll be with you all the way." "I will never leave you or forsake you." "I will light the way for you all the way." "I will never let you go through more troubles than you can bear through my grace and power." And He whispers so much more as I read and meditate on His Word. Praise the Lord!

I love to sing songs in my mind and heart that are totally based on God's Word. If a song is not based on the Bible or is contrary to God's Word, I have no use for it. I am so glad we don't sing such songs in our church. I especially

69

love to sing about Jesus. Songs about Jesus that I was taught as a child have permeated my thoughts all my life. Songs like, "Every day with Jesus is sweeter than the day before. Every day with Jesus I love Him more and more." And this old song about Jesus as the light, "The whole world was lost in the darkness of sin. The light of the world is Jesus."

Like sunshine at noon day His glory shone in. The light of the world is Jesus." As we really follow Jesus we are the light of the world. In Matthew 5:14 Jesus tells us as His disciples, "You are the light of the world – like a city on a mountain, glowing in the night for all to see." He then tells us to let our lights shine brightly so that people can see what God does for us and would do for them, and bring glory to our Father in heaven. Jesus lives in the world and gives light in darkness through us, His children. In Him we are the light of the world. The indication is there is no other. Jesus has given us His peace and light. It is in us. We are to let it shine. Yes, I also remember that little song I learned as a child, "This little light of mine, I'm going to let it shine." Let's "let it shine 'til Jesus comes."

It is indeed the light of the Lord Jesus shining in us that leads to life and peace. The darkness of the world leads to death. As children of God we are to walk in the light of Jesus. Studies have shown that people who are exposed to more physical light are more alive and even live longer. Even more so do we need to walk in the light of the Lord Jesus to be living, glowing, radiating

Christians in a world of darkness and sin. Then God wants us to have fellowship with others who walk in His light. God wants us to be the light to each other as His children so we can be one great shining light for Him for all the world to see.

Prayer: "Dear Lord Jesus, You are the light of the world. You have given to us eternal life and peace. You live in each of us and we are one together with you. You have chosen to make us the light of the world by living in and shining in us. We must live and walk in your light to make it through the darkness of this lost world. But you have us here to not just make it through, but to shine for you so people can see your light and come to it for life. I pray that you will shine brightly through me. I pray that in these dark times you will shine brightly through your church here and around the world."

REFLECTIONS:

_____

_____

_____

_____

_____

_____

_____

_____

_____

_____

_____

_____

_____

_____

_____

_____

PEACE MEANS KNOWING NOTHING CAN SEPARATE US FROM GOD

Romans 8:38-39, *"And I am convinced that nothing can separate us from His love. Death can't, and life can't. The angels can't, and the demons can't. Our fears for today, our worries about tomorrow, and even the powers of hell can't keep God's love away. Whether we are high above the sky or in the deepest ocean, nothing in all creation will ever be able to separate us from the love of God that is revealed in Christ Jesus our Lord."*

To say that nothing can separate us from God's love is to say that nothing can separate us from God. The Bible says in 1 John 4:16 that *"God is love."* When Paul says *"nothing can separate us from His love"* he is referring to "us" who have been born again and are now children of God. We are convinced as Paul was that nothing can separate us from God's love if we've trusted totally in Jesus and we belong to Him. In John 10:28-30 Jesus said of us, *"I give them eternal life, and they will never perish. No one will snatch them away from me, for my Father has given them to me, and He is more powerful than anyone else. No one can take them away from me. The Father and I are one."*

Everything that God says to us is in His Son, Jesus Christ. Because we belong to Him and He is our Lord we have eternal life in Him. We don't have to fear death because He has already defeated it. We don't have to fear life and all its pitfalls because we have the power of His resurrection to live victoriously. We thank Him for the angels He sends to attend and protect us. They are only powerful because they are from God. The demons are powerful and aim to defeat us, but God controls them, too.

We are still human and have those fears for today and worries about tomorrow. Praise God when we get to Heaven we will not have those fears and worries, but we are not there yet and this world is a battlefield. In the flesh we have every reason to be afraid and to worry. But The Holy Spirit living in us reassures us, comforts us and empowers us. As true followers of Jesus we are to walk in His Spirit. Since God is omnipresent, no matter where we are He is there with His love for us. When we walk in His Spirit not only do we not have to fear or worry; we rejoice in confident assurance of total victory in Jesus. I really love the following line from Isaac Watt's old hymn, "When I Can Read My Title Clear:" "Should Earth against my soul engage And fiery darts be hurled, Then I can smile at Satan's rage And face a frowning world."

And Yes, the powers of hell are strong. But Jesus said in Matthew 16:18 that all the powers of Hell will not conquer His Church because we are on the Rock, Jesus Christ. I know I am one of God's children. By His grace I am forgiven and I belong to Him. The God who is the creator and controller of the whole universe loves me and keeps me safe. I like it that even though Paul listed everything or power that we think could possibly separate us from God's love, he then indicated that if there was anything he may have left out, that too, could not do it. Here I say as I do often in thinking of these verses, "Praise the Lord."

Prayer: "Dear Lord, it is so wonderful to know you and your unfailing love. Thank you that you will never let anything separate me from you. After years of dealing with fears and worries I still have them sometimes. But I always go to your Word and talk to you about them. And you've never stopped loving me and you never will. Oh, for grace to trust you more. You are with me and love me in all the places and circumstances of my life. You never let go. I have all I need and more in Jesus Christ, my Lord."

We are still human and have those fears for today and worries about tomorrow. Praise God when we get to Heaven we will not have them but, we are not there yet and this world is a battlefield.

REFLECTIONS:

_____

_____

_____

_____

_____

_____

_____

_____

_____

_____

_____

_____

_____

_____

_____

_____

REFLECTIONS:

PEACE IN KNOWLEDGE THAT MY FUTURE IS IN GOD'S HANDS

Psalm 31:14-15, *"But I am trusting you, O Lord, saying, "You are my God!" My future is in your hands. Rescue me from those who hunt me down relentless."*

David was going through many dangers, sufferings and difficulties. In describing his hardships he said his friends would not even come near him. When they saw him coming down the street they would walk by on the other side. Others were conspiring to kill him, many were saying terrible things about him and many who knew about his plight just ignored him. But David said he was not trusting in people and the things of this world anyhow. He said they, are not my God. They cannot rescue me or destroy me. He believed that he belonged to God and nothing or nobody could hurt him. David knew that for anything or anybody to harm him or kill him they would have to go through God. To those today who are in Christ Jesus, we know that, too.

This verse and many similar verses have been a great comfort to me for many years. All of us have thought about when we may die. The Bible says there is that appointed time for each of us. It seems to me that most people don't die when they think they might. There are so many things that could take us out. For those who trust in God there are many enemies that would like to destroy us. And they are capable of doing so except for one thing. Even as David said it was for him, our futures are in God's hands. I will not die one moment sooner

79

than when God is ready for me to. Whenever that time comes I am fully prepared and will be ready to go to my eternal home. The knowledge and assurance that you belong to God is what gives you that peace and security.

Well, sometimes it might be easier to just die and go to our eternal home rather than to go through some of the difficulties, calamities and sufferings we may face. But for these, too, our times are in God's strong and loving hands. Sometimes God's people get into trouble and even for doing what is right. I've heard that in our time there are more Christians in the world facing persecution for their faith than in any other period of history. For most of these we may never know about them here. Just this week we learned of eight Christian workers who were killed in Afghanistan. Those claiming responsibility said they were killed for trying to spread their faith and had Bibles with them. I have often said that I'd rather be in trouble, danger and suffering while serving my Lord in His will for me, than to live in luxury and ease and be out of God's will.

On several occasions in my service for God and ministry to people I remember my life was threatened or being threatened. I confess that I was a bit uneasy about it at first. Then I remembered God's promise to take care of me and had great peace. I also remember thinking of the line in Martin Luther's hymn "A Mighty Fortress Is Our God" that says, "The body they may kill, God's truth abideth still. His kingdom is forever." I didn't like to think of my body being killed, but I had perfect peace knowing God was in control. We are joyful, happy and at peace as we submit to God's plan for our lives.

Prayer: "O Lord, through the years of my life, too often I have given into fears and distress. But you always speak to me and bring me back into your wonderful peace. Through the years you have led me to trust you in my heart. I am still trusting you now and I know that by your grace I always will. I pray for grace to trust you more. You are my mighty, all powerful, loving God. I know I belong to you. You are the blessed controller of all things in my life. Lord Jesus, you are victor and you live in me. That's all I need to know. I give honor, glory and praise to You. I want to live to show others your peace."

Even as David said it was for him, our futures are in God's hands. I will not die one moment sooner than when God is ready for me to.

REFLECTIONS:

REFLECTIONS:

_____

_____

_____

_____

_____

_____

_____

_____

_____

_____

_____

_____

_____

_____

_____

ROCK OF AGES, PEACE FOR ME

Psalm 62:5-7, *"I wait quietly before God, for my hope is in Him. He alone is my rock and my salvation, my fortress where I will not be shaken. My salvation and my honor come from God alone. He is my refuge, a rock where no enemy can reach me."*

David writes these words when he is once again in the midst of very difficult circumstances in his life. He trusted in God and had great comfort and strength as we do when we rely wholly on the same great God. David had said that at this time he had many enemies and all trying to destroy his life and influence. He said he was worth nothing to them, they planned to cause him to lose his job, they lied about him and all the while they pretended to be his friends.

In Psalm 3:5 David had said that even though he had these powerful enemies he had such peace that," I lay down and slept. I woke up in safety; for the Lord was watching over me." So, here is how to be able to sleep at night and go about your appointed work in the day no matter what may be happening or what you think may happen in your life.

David was saying, "Oh God, here is how it is. You know more about it than I do. I am trusting in you and believe you will do the right thing. I will rest and have peace and hope only in you." Throughout the Psalms David describes his various and many adversaries. He sometimes bemoans his lot in life and even complains to God. But he always concludes by expressing trust and praise to God. I still love the old hymn that begins, "Rock of ages, cleft for me. Let me hide myself in thee." Even as David did, you and I can hide, be secure and have sweet peace in the cleft of the great, solid, eternal Rock of ages. We know that our Lord Jesus is the Rock. He is the eternal foundation of our eternal life. He is the foundation for His Church. And nothing, not even "the gates of hell" can prevail against Him.

As children of our sovereign God we agree with David that He is the solid Rock on which we stand and cannot fall. He is our salvation for eternity and for all our life on Earth. We know now that eternal salvation is in Jesus, God's Son. He is our fortress. Enemies have to go through Him to get to us. It will never happen!

David was testifying that His salvation didn't come from anything he did, or didn't do. He gave total credit to God. It was the same for David's honor. He was honored in many ways by many people in the world. He said that he had real honor and it came only from God. And even as for us today, his peace and security was only in God.

In the following verses in Psalm 62 David encouraged the people in verse 8 to *"trust in God at all times,"* and to *"pour out your hearts to him."* In verse 10 he exhorts them to not try to get rich, but to just do your job as a servant and if you do get wealth don't center in or trust in it. Peace and power is not in wealth. In verse 11 David said what we all need to often be reminded of:

"God has spoken plainly, and I have heard it many times: Power, Oh God, belongs to you."

Prayer: "Dear Lord, I can pray as David did: I wait quietly before you, for my hope is in you. You alone are my Rock and my salvation, my fortress where I will not be shaken. My salvation and my honor come from you alone. You are my refuge, a rock where no enemy can reach me. And I thank you that by your grace I can say without doubt that you are my peace, my eternal Rock of ages.

REFLECTIONS:

_____

_____

_____

_____

_____

_____

_____

_____

_____

_____

_____

_____

_____

_____

_____

_____

PEACE IN SUBMISSION TO GOD'S WONDERFUL PLAN

Jeremiah 1:4-5, *"The Word of the Lord came to me saying, before I formed you in the womb I knew you, before you were born I set you apart; I appointed you as a prophets to the nations."* NIV

When God called Jeremiah to serve Him, Jeremiah at first rebelled. He made the same typical excuses that are made today for not serving God. Jeremiah said, "I can't do it." God said, "You are right. You can't, but I can and I have chosen to use you to do it." Jeremiah's problem and his response to God was fear. God would turn his human fear into reverential fear and respect for Him, the awesome all-powerful God who is in control and in authority of all the world.

The peace of God begins with a receptive and submissive heart to "The Word of the Lord." Though Jeremiah at first did not like what God told him to do, he did continue to listen to the Word of the Lord and because he had a heart for God, he submitted. The Bible says in Proverbs 1:7, "Fear of the Lord is the beginning of knowledge. Only fools despise wisdom and discipline." No one can really know and understand anything until he comes to the place of reverential fear, respect and humility before our awesome, wonderfully great God.

I don't really believe Jeremiah enjoyed much of the work God gave him to do. He did have the joy of the Lord, the knowledge that God would be in control, be with him and take care of him. He believed God's word to him was true and he knew the outcome would be glorious and victorious. God has a wonderful plan for each of our lives. In submitting to God and His plan for us we have the same assurance Jeremiah had. Before God formed each of us in the womb He knew us. Before we were born we were set apart. He appointed us to serve Him now, where we are.

God has a special plan and place for each of His followers. He never lets go of us. He never stops loving us. He never loves us less. Oh what peace we have to know we are owned and loved by Him. Nothing that ever happens to us is ever a surprise to God. He is not the author of confusion and turmoil, but He knew it would happen and knows He is going to lead us through it in victory, even as He did for Jeremiah. And as Paul said in Romans 8:18, *"Yet what we suffer now is nothing to the glory he will give us later."*

Prayer: "Dear Lord, I don't think I could face life's journey in this turbulent world without submitting to your control and authority. You daily assure me of your presence and power for whatever may happen. As you told Jeremiah, you tell me often that any effort to defeat me will fail, "For I am with you and will take care of you. I, the Lord, have spoken." (Jeremiah 1:19) Thank you again for your wonderful plan and purpose for my life."

Nothing that ever happens to us is ever a surprise to God. He is not the author of confusion and turmoil, but He knew it would happen and knows He is going to lead us through it in victory, even as He did for Jeremiah.

REFLECTIONS:

_____

_____

_____

_____

_____

_____

_____

_____

_____

_____

_____

_____

_____

_____

_____

_____

GOD'S PLAN FOR US IS PEACE

Jeremiah 29:11, *"For I know the plans I have for you, "says the Lord." They are for good and not disaster, to give you a future and a hope."*

These words are in the letter Jeremiah wrote to downcast Jews who had been exiled to Babylon. Jeremiah encouraged them in his letter to work for and pray for peace and prosperity where they were. He tells them that if they lived among a people who had peace they too would have peace. They were encouraged to make the best of their situation and to trust God to take care of them.

Jeremiah tells them not to listen to the naysayers, the false prophets and the mediums who were trying to discourage them. He says they were lying to them and they don't speak for the Lord.
The Lord is really telling them through His prophet Jeremiah that He has everything under control and that He has not forgotten them.

So often God speaks to me in His Word and by His Spirit and gives me a message of power and encouragement when I am wondering what is happening and why. He says I am to be still and listen to Him. In Psalm 1:1-2 God says, *"Oh the joy of those who do not follow the advice of the wicked, or stand around with sinners, or join in with scoffers. But they delight in doing everything the Lord wants; day and night they think about His law."*

These downcast Jews to whom Jeremiah was writing had lost everything of material and transient earthly value. Most freedoms they had formerly known had been taken from them. These are certainly uncertain and perilous times our nation is in today. We are in terrible economical times. And morally the nation is becoming bankrupt. We are not to bury our heads in the sand and act like it's not happening. But Jeremiah would tell us today, God doesn't want us to be in an attitude of doom and despair.

God is still on His throne and in control no matter what happens or what anyone says about it. Well, someone may say, "Try telling that to someone who is really affected by these current economically difficult times." Well yes, try to tell that to anyone who is going through sufferings, difficulties and hardships, and pray and hope they listen and trust more in our God who is in control as He always is.

Prayer: "Dear Lord, thank you for the great plan and purpose you have had for my life all along. You have certainly been so good to me and blessed me greatly, especially in tough times. I give honor, glory and praise all to you. You have a wonderful plan for my life for now and for the future. I have too often given into negative, pessimistic thoughts of defeat. They never happened. My hope is only in you and my future is secure as it is for all who follow You. Your goodness and mercy has and will follow me all the days of my life and I will always live with you.

REFLECTIONS:

_____

_____

_____

_____

_____

_____

_____

_____

_____

_____

_____

_____

_____

_____

_____

PEACE IN SUFFERING

2 Corinthians 12:8-9, *"Three times I begged the Lord to take it away. Each time He said, 'My gracious favor is all you need. My power works best for your weakness.' So now I am glad to boast about my weaknesses, so that the power of Christ may work through me."*

Paul had just come from a mountain top spiritual experience with the Lord. God specially blessed Paul in giving him such a wonderful experience of visions and revelation. He said he believed the experience was something worth boasting about. But he said he would rather talk about how God would use him most in his weaknesses. God allowed him to have what Paul called "a thorn in his flesh." Whatever it was it was probably painful and was very much troublesome to Paul. He prayed three times for the Lord to take it away. The Lord Jesus told him each time that he would give Paul all he needed in grace and strength.

Paul said the weaknesses in the flesh were things he could and would boast about because they would certainly give glory and praise to the Lord and that was what he lived for. Real prayer is submission to God and brings acceptance of real grace and the peace of God. The indication here is that Paul accepted the thorn in the flesh as God's will for him for then. Real prayer leads to being submissive to God's will for our lives no matter what happens.

I believe that Paul would pray, "Lord, thank you for hearing and answering my prayers. Thank you for blessing me and for using me to bless others by your grace and power." Such submission brings peace like a river flowing in and through your soul. It did for Paul. It will for us. Fanny J. Crosby, the great hymn writer of many years ago was blind most of her life. I think she expressed Paul's sentiments to God's answer to his prayer in a verse from her great hymn, "Blessed Assurance", "Perfect submission, all is at rest, I in my Savior am happy and blest, Watching and waiting, looking above, filled with His goodness, lost in His love."

Why was Paul so willing to go through and even delighted in all kinds of suffering and weaknesses for Christ? In verse 10 he said, *"For when I am weak, then I am strong."* It was really because Paul's hearts desire to God as stated in Romans 10:1 was "that the Jewish people might be saved." Paul came to have the same heart's desire for the Gentiles and for all people. He was willing to endure any hardship for his heart's desire. Some hardships he endured were shipwreck, beaten, imprisoned, run out of town and stoned, betrayed by friends and hated. In all his life God's power did work mightily through Paul.

Prayer: "Dear Lord, thank you for always hearing and answering my prayers according to your will and grace for me. Thank you that when I am weak, then I have your real strength to serve you and do your will. Thank you for using me to bless others by your grace and power.

I am so weak, but you are so strong. May my heart's desire be for more people to be saved."

REFLECTIONS:

_____

_____

_____

_____

_____

_____

_____

_____

_____

_____

_____

_____

_____

_____

_____

_____

OVERFLOWING WITH GOD'S HOPE BRINGS JOY AND PEACE

Romans 15:13, *"So I pray that God, who gives you hope, will keep you happy and full of peace as you believe in Him. May you overflow with hope through the power of the Holy Spirit."*

Recently in a doctor's office when I was questioned about my physical health history I was asked, "Is there anything about your spiritual belief that influences your health?" I immediately replied, "Well, yes, my trust is totally in Jesus Christ as the forgiver of my sins and the Lord of my life. I believe that He is in control of my life and that influences everything. I have perfect peace in Him." That seemed to make the questioner uncomfortable for the moment and she continued the interview. But it is God only who gives us hope in any situation in this life. All other hope is false. I do believe in Him and have His joy and peace in me. God desires for each person to have this hope alive in him.

As I grow older I am more assured than ever that God's grace is all we need for these increasingly troubled times. I still must deal with the sinful human nature. But my life is controlled by the Spirit of God living in me. When I keep my mind fixed on my powerful, loving Lord I do not give into the worries, anxieties and concerns of the world. Then nothing but God's joy and perfect peace rules in my heart.

We know that there is no doubt according to God's Word that God loves all people. We are all special to Him and loved by Him. He *"so loved the world."* Jewish people are special to Him as His chosen people. All who believe and receive Jesus are His chosen people and are special to Him. As God's dear children it is only God our eternal Father who gives us peace and joy in all the times of our lives.

In Romans 15 Paul encourages the Roman Christians to have a spirit of unity in following Jesus Christ. He says that Christ is the ruler over all of us and all of us together should give glory to God. The prayer of Paul in verse 13 is for individual Christians and for the body of believers in Rome. It is also meant as prayer in the same way for us today. God has from the beginning always been in control. He is our only true, awesome God and our hope is in Him forever. We should accept this prayer for assurance and peace now and pray it for others.

Our hope is given to us forever and the assurance of it is renewed each day from God the Holy Spirit in us. We know we belong to God and that He keeps us. He wants to keep us in His peace and joy each day. He wants us to be full of His peace so that it will be for everything that happens in our lives. He wants His peace and hope to overflow from us into the lives of others we are in contact with each day. As we bless others, hope in Christ will overflow and come back to us multiplied in abundance. It is the fullness of the power of the Holy Spirit within us that gives this assurance to us and others. We are to pray each day to be filled with the awareness of the Holy Spirit's presence and power.

Prayer: "We pray that you, the God of hope, will fill each of us and all of us with joy and peace. We pray that we will trust you totally and obey you. Give us hope that overflows into others around us by the power of the Holy Spirit. We want to live each day to bring praise, honor and glory to you."

REFLECTIONS:

_____

_____

_____

_____

_____

_____

_____

_____

_____

_____

_____

_____

_____

_____

_____

_____

PEACE IN OUR ONENESS IN CHRIST

Ephesians 2:14, *"For Christ Himself has made peace between us Jews and you Gentiles by making us all one people. He has broken down the wall of hostility that used to separate us."*

You may believe it and receive it, or not, but the Bible makes it clear that the only way to knowing God and having peace with God is through His Son, Jesus Christ. In Ephesians 2:13 Paul made it clear that before we knew Jesus we were far from God and now that we know Him and forgiveness of sins through His sacrificial death for us, we belong to God.

When Christ is our savior and Lord He is the Lord of Peace in our lives. We are one together with our Lord who gives us peace. His presence, power and peace dominate all of our lives. We are one together with others of all backgrounds who have also received peace with God through Jesus. A most wonderful and even miraculous thing to see among Christians is how God takes many people of many different backgrounds and blends them together as one harmonious unit. It does not take away the different
personalities, likes, dislikes and character differences of people.

God's perfect love binds us all together in His love, joy, peace and power. It really is the fulfillment of our Lord's prayer in John 17:2021, *"I am praying not only for these disciples but also for all who will ever believe in me because of their testimony. My prayer for all of them is that they will be one, just as you and I are one, Father – that just as you are in me and I in you, so they will be in us, and the world will know you sent me."*

Before we knew Christ we were separated by "the wall of hostility." Now each of us and all of us together are one in worshipping and serving our Lord Jesus. Our common purpose is that the world may know Jesus. That common purpose supersedes everything else. We are in the same kingdom – His, on the same team – His, in the same family – His, on the same page – with Him, and headed for the same place – His Heaven.

It is most important that we make sure that the focus of attention in our church, Bible study groups, and assemblies be on Jesus. When it is not, "the wall of hostility" can begin to build. Then sins of the flesh, greed, envy, selfishness and other hostilities begin to be in control. It is when people begin to want their own way. They forget their purpose in Christ. They begin to lose His peace that comes only with submission to His control. When we submit to His control the fruits of His Spirit are present. Read them and memorize them in Galatians 5:22.

Prayer: "Dear Lord, may I constantly look to you for peace. There is no place else to go. You alone have the Words of life and peace. You want your peace to rule in me. And, above all other places and people in the world your church is to be where your peace reigns. We know it is, when You are in control. You are not the author of confusion or disorder. We ask you to never let that wall of hostility build in our fellowship of those who follow you in the purpose that the world may know you are the Christ. You have promised that as long as we stay in that purpose your presence will assure that the fellowship of sweet peace will continue."

REFLECTIONS:

PEACE THAT KEEPS US FROM FALLING

Psalm 37:23-24, *"The steps of the Godly are directed by the Lord. He delights in every detail of their lives. Though they stumble, they will not fall, for the Lord holds them by the hand."*

Those who are Godly are not perfect, except in God. They have a heart for God and trust in Him. Their heart's desire is to walk in God's way. They have sought Him and found Him as their Savior and Master. Now they seek to know Him better and to serve Him. They take delight in the Lord. The Lord takes "delight in every detail of their lives." They delight in knowing the Lord directs and protects their steps. They know the Lord delights in their lives, even when they stumble. They are God's dear children, growing in the grace and knowledge of their Lord. And children do stumble and fall. God's children stumble but God does not let them fall and stay down.

So, why do God's children not fall when they stumble? We become God's children by accepting His Son Jesus for the forgiveness of our sins and as the leader of our lives. God does not stumble. He does not fall. We do stumble, but He does not let us fall. Why? As we walk, He directs our steps and holds our hand. These verses do not say the Godly hold God's hand. It says He holds our hand. When we lose our grip He doesn't lose His.

109

When each of our four sons were babies I looked forward to taking them for walks. I taught them to walk with attention and delight. They also learned how to fall. But when I held their hands they did not fall. When I first took our first son, Tim, for a walk on the sidewalk I decided to see how fast he could walk. We soon walked faster than he could go and he started to fall. Of course he didn't fall because I held his little hand firmly. I said out loud, "Praise the Lord" because these verses came to my mind. I praise Him that though I stumble often He never lets me fall and never will.

Godly people are constantly being attacked by the devil. We are weak and when we take our eyes off Jesus we will begin to fall and sink even as Peter did when he was walking on the water. But the Godly will not stay down. In Proverbs 4:15 Solomon warns evil doers to not try to hurt the Godly. And in verse 16 he says the Godly "may trip seven times, but each time they will rise again. But one calamity is enough to lay the wicked low." Years ago I heard someone say, "When you're flat on your back there is only one direction you can look." I also heard, "falling down does not make you a failure, but staying down does." Even then if you are Godly in your heart for God, He will lift you back up. When Dwight Eisenhower was asked what he thought was the difference between great men and ordinary men, he replied, "Great men, when they get down, always get back up." Actually that is the difference between the Godly and the ungodly. But it is God Himself who lifts the Godly up.

Prayer: Dear Lord, thank you for giving me a heart for you. Thank you that you have directed my steps through my life. I know that you love me and care about every detail of my life. You delight in me because I am your child. Thank you for holding my hand and even increasing your grip when I let go for awhile. I am a winner because you are the Victor." "Oh no, you never let go, in every high, in every low. Oh no, you never let go. Lord you never let go of me."*

*from the song, "Oh no, You Never Let Go," by Matt and Beth Redman. Often when praying I burst forth singing a certain song.

REFLECTIONS:

THE PEACE OF GOD EXPRESSED IN JOY

Proverbs 15:13, *"A wise heart makes a happy face; a broken heart crushes the spirit."* Proverbs 17:22, *"A cheerful heart is good medicine, but a broken spirit saps a person's strength."*

I've always believed that having the peace of God, being led by the Spirit and having a good time (having fun) do go together very appropriately. Those who served on staff in churches where I have been pastor sometimes have reminded me that when there was pressure and a tendency to be uptight I would say in staff meetings, "Okay, let's just lighten up, relax and have a good time." Then I would tell a humorous story (I thought so) and let them share some. This, with prayer and trusting God would take away tension and bring peace and calm.

A wise heart is one that trusts God no matter what happens. God gives peace in the midst of storms when we trust Him. When one has the peace of God in His heart it may not show in his face at first, but it soon will. When a heart is broken the spirit is crushed. But the broken heart that turns to God in child like trust will be healed. I once heard someone say, "If you have the joy and peace of the Lord in your heart you should inform your face." If you really have the joy of the Lord in your heart your face will show it.

Solomon says that joy heals. Healing is so needed in many lives, homes and even churches today. What will do it? The joy of the Lord will do it. The joy of the Lord

113

is the very best heart medicine and it is free.   It is prescribed here in Proverbs 17:22 by the Lord.   Healing will take place when there is joyful walking and talking, joyful conversations, joyful preaching, joyful teaching, joyful singing, joyful giving, joyful testifying, joyful witnessing, joyful   serving, joyful praising God, and continual "rejoicing in the Lord always."

In Proverbs 16:33 Solomon says, "From a wise man comes wise speech; the words of the wise are persuasive."   A person with his heart right with God will speak about it with joy.   He has the joy of the Lord and it gives persuasiveness.   We've all heard those who usually speak what is right, but with an unwise attitude. I've heard some speak at meetings and though I agreed with what they were saying I wished they would keep quiet since their words were not being accepted because of their attitude.

When my pastor friend Lee Feeler was in the hospital in Cheyenne, Wyoming he sent word that he wanted me to come to see him soon that day.   In our conversations in serving the Lord together Lee and I often helped each other see the lighter side of things.   That day when I walked into his room Lee said, "Paul, I have good news and bad news and I'll tell you the good news first.   I'm going to get to see Jesus before you do."   We both smiled and even chuckled.   His spirit was just fine. Proverbs 18:14 says, "The human spirit can endure a sick body, but who can bear it if the spirit is crushed?"   I left

Lee's room with tears of sorrow, but praising the Lord in peace and joy. Lee soon was well with Jesus.

Prayer: "Thank you for giving me so much to rejoice in your joy about through the years you've let me live and serve you. There has been a lot of sorrow, too. But, I thank you that even in the midst of troubles and pain you always give your joy. Help me to always communicate your Good News in joyful persuasiveness."

REFLECTIONS:

PEACE IN STORMS

Mark 4:39, *"And He arose, and rebuked the wind, and said unto the sea, Peace , be still. And the wind ceased, and there was a great calm."* KJV

This passage on peace has been a great help and blessing to me since my childhood. I am sure it has for many of you, too. In fact when I think of it I still remember it in the King James Version which I have printed here. I have meditated on it many times when I felt the storms of life raging in my life. I still meditate on it for the storms that come in this time of life.

My usual response when storms come into my life is something like the disciples reaction in this passage. I instinctively go to the Lord. I call on Him for help but too often it is in fear and panic. The disciples said, "Teacher, don't you even care that we are going to drown?" Jesus as the Son of God in human flesh was asleep. But God was not asleep. He never grows tired and never sleeps. He is always watching over each of His own to take care of us.

Jesus arose, undisturbed by the storm. He rebuked the storm and said, "Peace, be still." I wish I could have been there to see and experience that. In one moment the boat appears about to be destroyed. In the next moment everything becomes perfectly still and quiet. What a change. What a miracle. What perfect peace. I've seen and felt that change and peace often when I've called on God in the midst of storms in my life and in others as we called on Him. Jesus reminded His disciples then that He had always been in control of the storm and they needed to learn to trust Him for all the storms that would come.

When the storms of life are raging we have an anchor. We who have given our hearts to Jesus serve a Savior who will, in a moment, cause us to have a peace and calm that no one else or nothing else can give.   In 2 Corinthians 4:8 Paul said that we who trust the risen Savior, *"are pressed on every side by troubles, but we are not crushed and broken. We are perplexed, but we don't give up and quit. We are hunted down, but God never abandons us. We get knocked down, but we get up again and keep going."*

These disciples learned that Jesus loved them and cared deeply about what happens to them. He didn't keep on sleeping. He didn't tell them to just shut up and calm down. He didn't just impatiently jump up and dismiss the storm. He hushed the storm so the fearful disciples wouldn't miss the response and the lesson.   He then reminded them that they wouldn't be afraid in any storm when they learned to just trust in Him. So, peace during a storm comes by knowing God's Word. Read it, pray it, meditate on it, listen to it proclaimed, study it in small groups and in all this, share His Word and His peace with others. You really know it is a vital part of you when you find yourself sharing the overflow.

The disciples learned great lessons here and I pray that you and I won't miss them. They learned that Jesus is with each of His followers at all times. His love and care is revealed to us even more meaningful when the storms of life are raging the most fierce. And He will be there when we face our greatest enemy, death. As Christian what shall we lose when we die? Nothing, compared with what we shall gain. And this means that since we are not afraid to die and leave this world behind we are really ready to live in it until we do.

There are many more lessons in this peace passage. I must mention one more here. Christ's first Church was on board this small boat. There was no way it was going to be destroyed. Christ is always present with His Church for her protection and deliverance. She goes through the fires. He is always there. She goes through storms. He is always there. PRAISE THE LORD!

Prayer: "Dear Lord, we thank you and praise you for all those times you stilled the raging storms in our lives. Thank you for being patient with us in our panic and lack of greater trust in you. Help us to face the future storms with confident trust in you to take us through them with assurance of victory in your presence and power. Thank you for your patience and power in our church. We know it is your church and will not be defeated. All glory and praise to you."

His love and care is revealed to us even more meaningful when the storms of life are raging the most fierce.

REFLECTIONS:

_____

_____

_____

_____

_____

_____

_____

_____

_____

_____

_____

_____

_____

_____

_____

_____

REFLECTIONS:

PEACE IN GOD'S PURPOSE FOR OUR LIVES

Romans 8:28, *"And we know that God causes everything to work together for the good of those who love God and are called according to His purpose for them."*

This precious promise of God has given me peace and greatly blessed my life since I first came to know Jesus as my savior and leader. I know it and understand it and am filled with praise to God in its application to my life. Yet it is difficult to explain how I know it since almost every time I read and meditate on this chapter in Romans I see things of blessing that it seems I never saw before. And there is so much in it, that it is hard to put it into a few words. Well, any time I speak or write comments on verses in the Bible I pray that others will listen and be inspired to study it deeper for application to their own lives.

It is paramount to note that in this verse and in all the Bible we are told that God has a purpose for each person who is chosen and called by God to follow Him. And the purpose is always good. God's purpose for each of His children is that we become more like Jesus and walk with Him daily. It is that we be conformed to His image and have the mind of Christ in our walk with Him. I often find myself singing the first verse of the song, "Be Thou My Vision." I sing these words in my paraphrase, "Lord be my vision, be king of my heart. Nothing else matters except that you are. Please guide my thinking

123

by day and by night. Awaking or sleeping, your presence my light." When we love our Lord that is the way we want it to be in our lives.

The key words in Romans 8:28 is "his purpose." The promise is that God will see that all things work together for the good of those who love Him and are called and committed to His purpose for them. We know that the Bible teaches that God has a plan and purpose for the lives of each individual Christian. But the purpose of God that Paul refers to in this promise is the same for all who are truly His children. I have never heard this promise quoted with verse 29 included. You can't get the meaning without including it. When you believe it, know it is true and meditate on it, you have all the peace and comfort you need for any situation in life. I hope you read it in your own Bible but here it is: *"For God knew His people in advance, and He chose them to become like His Son, so that His Son would be the firstborn, with many brothers and sisters."*

I don't know why God chose me to be His child. I don't know why He called me to become like Christ - a Christian. I know I'm not perfect like Jesus yet. But I know that I am like Him in that I have been born again and am now God's child. I know without doubt that I love Him with all my heart and I desire to serve Him and to honor Him in all I do. And Paul says that not only does God know His children, but that He knew in advance we would be.

Our purpose as Christians in this world is to become more like Jesus every day and in every way. The purpose is that Jesus is in the world living in each of His children. So, as we follow Jesus His Spirit in us will remind us through His Word of what the purpose of Jesus is in the world. It is the way of peace in the life of each Christian and in the life of each church. The purpose of God in the world is to save His children. In Luke 19:10 Jesus, referring to salvation coming to Zacchaeus, said, *"And I, the Son of Man, have come to seek and save those like Him, who are lost."* He was lost before He met and believed in Jesus, as is everybody in the world today. That purpose of Jesus in the world and His followers in the world, is taught throughout the Bible.

How God's purpose is fulfilled will vary from Christian to Christian and from Church to Church. But it is to be the same and the very heart of life for us all. God tells us in 2 Corinthians 5:20 that we are His ambassadors and it is though Christ Himself were pleading for the salvation of people through us. In being like Jesus, God's purpose in each of our lives is that we have His peace, joy, love and all the fruits of His Spirit. He wants us to enjoy life to the fullest in all the circumstances that come. He tells us that He will see to it that it all works together for our good. In everything that happens He wants us to reach out with the good news of salvation in Jesus to everyone who will listen.

Prayer: "Dear Lord, thank you for the peace you give us daily knowing that nothing that happens in our lives is meaningless and our lives have purpose, your purpose. We want to submit daily and joyfully to your purpose for us. We know you will use it all to bring us closer to you and to become more like you. We thank you for calling us, choosing us and living in us. We want to live and enjoy life to the fullest. We want it all to bring honor and glory to you."

> # God's purpose for each of His children is that we become more like Jesus and walk with Him daily.

REFLECTIONS:

REFLECTIONS: